COFFEE

COFFEE

FOR WHEN YOUR GET-UP-AND-GO HAS GONE!

CARL MAINWARING

Copyright © 2012 MESNIL WARIN Publishing

ISBN: 978-0-473-62830-7

Published by: Mesnil Warin Publishing, a division of ARIVII LTD, 88 Krippner Road, Puhoi, Auckland, 0953, New Zealand.

FIRST EDITION KNOWLEDGE SERIES: COFFEE

SOFTCOVER - POB: ISBN: 978-0-473-62830-7

HARDCOVER - POB: ISBN 978-0-473-62831-4

EPUB: ISBN 978-0-473-62832-1

KINDLE: ISBN 978-0-473-62833-8

APPLE BOOKS: ISBN 978-0-473-62834-5

TO COFFEE LOVERS EVERYWHERE.

Let's put the go back in your get-up-and-go!

DEDICATED

Jim Broadbent

I dedicated this book to Jim Broadbent of Kerikeri, a good friend. Jim was born of a world of chivalry that he practiced so well, the ever gentleman who always put others before himself. I owe an outstanding debt of gratitude to Jim, who gave me the wisdom to see the good in people.

Jim and coffee went together. We spent many a morning in one of the many coffee houses of Kerikeri with other colleagues and friends, drinking coffee, people watching, and generally talking twaddle with occasional hints of intelligent conversation. It's with a tear and a smile; I recall the many happy times, laugh or cry, or a bit of both. Oh, how I miss those mornings.

This book is for you, Jim; I'm sure you are sitting with the big guy upstairs. I can see you now in that little coffee house on the corner, looking out to the pearly gates with a coffee in one hand, chatting and laughing. Thank you, Jim, for being a friend and a confidant, bringing laughter into my life, and giving me and many others a sense of life. You may be gone, but you will always live on in my heart and the hearts of the many thousands of souls you touched. This one's for you!

COFFEE

TABLE OF CONTENT

INTRODUCTION:

"Rest and Relaxation"

Today, I planned to have my rest day, but the universe had an alternative plan in mind for me. My phone rang, and there it was, a so-called emergency. We've all had them; oh well, here we go again! However, this turned out to be one of my best days for discovery. Navigating through the city office blocks using an overzealous sat nav that I call Margret (sorry to all the Margarets), I came across this single-story quaint coffee house surrounded by Pohutukawa trees (New Zealand Christmas trees) with beautiful red flowers hidden amongst a towering concrete jungle. It was pretty surreal, but what a pleasure. Tenderly, I went inside and ordered my favorite beverage, a long black, always double shot and always with a side of hot water. Would it meet my high expectations? So, resetting the scene, my planned rest day turned out to be just that.

When the smooth, rich, earthy scent of fresh coffee is in the air, most of us cannot help but feel relaxed. While coffee runs through your body, increasing your heartbeat just a little, the calmness of the environment, coupled with the smell and taste

of that perfect coffee, slows the world down; it's as if you are in some alternative universe, the good place. Coffee has been around for centuries, captivating people's minds across all backgrounds and cultures. It is the mainstay of many economic exports for many countries, with countries such as Brazil producing nearly 53 million bags of coffee every year. There are infinite ways to enjoy coffee, ranging from espresso to cappuccino. On top of all that, the world consumes 2.24 billion cups of coffee daily each year. So, what is the deal with this simple drink? If you are interested in this book, it is worth assuming that you have a fascination for coffee. Perhaps you're asking yourself, where is coffee grown? What is the best way to drink it? How did cafes come to be? And why is coffee just so good?

This book will give you the know-how to rival the experts on all things coffee, giving you an in-depth understanding of everything relating to this humble drink. From how coffee was first discovered to how we love to consume it, you will learn the different flavor profiles of Arabica and Robusta coffee and how to narrow down which one you might prefer. You will read about the long history of coffee and its placement in political activism. By the end of this book, you will know how to find your favorite brewing method and how it compliments certain types of coffee. This book consists of five chapters. From the origin of the first-ever coffee bean consumed to the many health benefits, giving you the know-how to identify the many various aromas and subtle taste differences from other coffee growing regions in the world.

The first chapter begins with the basics, the history of coffee houses, from discovering the coffee plant in Ethiopia or Yemen (depending on whom you ask) to how we experience coffee houses today. It looks at how coffee was influential and pivotal in all societies it touched due to its accessibility to those of all social standings. Coffee houses quickly became much more than an establishment to drink coffee, evolving into social change powerhouses in many countries where coffee was popular. This chapter also looks at how coffee has not always been the loved social stimulus that it is today. With open political discussions of dissent, coffee houses were a magnet for overthrowing the political elite, leading to the banning of coffee in several countries! The dramatic history of coffee houses is undoubtedly not one to be missed.

Chapter two looks at the health benefits of coffee, particularly in its relation to polyphenols, compounds found in plants. Some polyphenols are known to be great for our health and are now extensively studied; they are even linked to slowing down the aging process. We will delve deep by looking at researched articles focused on the benefits coffee has on improving our bodies' largest organ, the skin, and how coffee is a great metabolism booster that can even help us lose weight without trying! We will also examine how coffee research is growing in fields such as brain health and disease prevention. There is evidence that coffee helps us retain our cognitive function and reduces our chances of developing cancers and other deadly illnesses.

Chapter three goes back to the heart of coffee itself, the land it is grown on. We review all areas of the coffee belt to delve deeper into the varieties of coffee and the flavor differences that arise from these regions. For example, did you know that coffee from Africa tends to be fruity and winey in its subtle flavors, while coffee from Thailand can taste like macadamia nuts? Each country has its practices and habits in growing coffee, which affect the flavor. So, this chapter examines the many aspects of producing coffee from around the world.

Chapter four works to apply the knowledge from the other chapters to your everyday life in the way of purchasing your own coffee. You have learned about the history, benefits, and varieties of coffee. It is now time to learn how to choose one by learning about the standard dimensions of coffee, such as noticing different flavors mentioned on coffee packaging. We also examine how to pair coffee with the numerous brewing methods to help you find the best combination to enjoy. You will see the benefits of buying from local roasters and how the internet grants you the option to try a range of fresh coffees without needing to leave your home. Finally, we look at the catchy words and certificates you may encounter in your coffee search to know which ones are legitimate and which ones are attempting to con you with fake quality.

The final chapter will look at how to create the perfect cup. Enjoying coffee differs between each individual. One hat does not fit all; we are individuals with individual tastes. We will explore the many aspects of different brewing options that you can choose from. We outline the best versions, why each of them has differing qualities, and where they may fall a little short. This way, you can apply all you have learned to explore and elevate your coffee experience, whether from your home or your favorite coffee shop. Coffee making is a craft, so each option takes a bit of time to perfect, but in the end, you will have learned a new skill and created a fantastic cup of coffee on an enriching and enjoyable journey.

Drinking coffee is not like drinking water; it is complex with a fascinating culture. Ask anyone you know, and you will receive differing answers about how and why they like coffee. But we can all agree that it is our favorite drink; why else would you be here? Let's delve further into coffee, from the inception of the coffee house, to where revolutionary ideas were hatched, to today's coffee culture; this is the fascinating and delicious coffee community that we partake in every day. So let's dive into the world of coffee and emerge on the other side with a better appreciation and understanding of our beloved cup of joe.

COFFEE

CHAPTER 1

HISTORY OF THE COFFEE HOUSES

"Café de la Paix"

One of the most significant elements of coffee is the atmosphere that surrounds it. When the aromatic scent of coffee fills the air, many people instantly feel as if they are in a relaxed and comforting space. The smell of coffee even entices people to get out of bed each morning, acting as a pick-me-up for a great

day ahead. Is this because coffee has some magical mystic power over us, or is it due to something else? Many would say it is because coffee tastes so good, but the sensations coffee brings should not be written off so quickly.

This chapter will cover the social origins of coffee and its effects on people and politics. The original coffee houses were not the ones we know today. Modern cafes are often tranquil, with comfy seats to sit and read, and enough outlets to power everyone's working computers. They have a quiet and cozy nature to them; this is why they are a favorite spot for studying or just catching up with an old friend. But the old coffee houses were packed, noisy, and chaotic, filled with people from all social standings and backgrounds, seated together as equals as they enjoyed the fine intellectual booster known as coffee.

Why such a difference from what we see now in a coffee house to the original coffee house? One answer might be the purpose and culture of the coffee house. This chapter will review the long history of coffee houses and their pivotal role in the society we live in today. From the inception of coffee and the coffee houses in the early Ottoman Empire, to its spread into Europe and across the sea to the Americas, to the coffee and cafes we all know and love today.

The Origin of Coffee and Coffee Houses - The Ottoman Empire

From what researchers understand, coffee consumption did not begin with the drink we know and love today, but by eating the coffee fruit itself. There is a legend about its discovery coming from Ethiopia. "One day, a goat farmer named Kaldi noticed that his goats were eating these small red berries from a nearby tree. The goats became so excited that they refused to sleep throughout the night. The farmer decided to try the berries for himself and was surprised to find that they gave him energy throughout long nights of prayer. Kaldi then told some nearby monks, who decided to burn the beans thinking they were creations of the devil. But after smelling their tempting aroma, they recovered the beans, crushed them into a powder, and drank them throughout the night" (Bigirimana, 1). "This legend is said to have taken place in 700 AD; many suspect coffee productions began before this" (Bigirimana, 1). The belief is that coffee originated in Ethiopia's Kaffa region and spread across the lands into the Arabian Peninsula, where its popularity grew even further. People learned how to perfect the crafting of coffee within their homes due to there being no designated public place to enjoy coffee for hundreds of years. Eventually, due to the drink's immense popularity, specialist coffee houses were constructed to serve coffee and offer an atmosphere to enjoy it.

Coffee houses as we know them began in the Ottoman empire. The long thriving empire was known as a hub for trade and culture, making it a natural place for social interaction and enjoyment of coffee. "Coffee roasting practices began in modern-day Yemen around 1200" (Suter, 107). They acted as professional places for the personal purchase of coffee in one's home. The spread of coffee is sometimes attributed to the Sufis, a mystic denomination of the Islamic religion, with some retellings of the Kaldi legend saying he shared the abilities of coffee with them instead. Another variation says that "Ebu'l Hassan Şazeli, the founder of the mystic Şazeli sect, reportedly first discovered coffee on a trip to Mecca in 1258. He then promoted coffee drinking from there and became the 'patron saint' of coffee houses" (Gamm, 1). Despite how the original myth varies, the discovery of coffee and the development of the humble coffee houses led to a cascade of social-cultural development.

Although coffee was well established throughout the Ottoman empire, it still took over two hundred years to create coffee houses; before this, the consumption of coffee had been limited to people's homes. "After centuries of coffee consumption, the first coffee house opened in Constantinople, now known as Istanbul, Turkey, in 1475" (Suter, 107). The humble coffee house was the start of the coffee culture, and very quickly, the coffee houses multiplied in Istanbul and around the Ottoman Empire. You may think this was because people loved the drink so much; while there is some truth in part, coffee houses served a much larger purpose than just distributing the humble cup of coffee; they were hubs for social activity and often social unrest!

People frequently gravitate to public places that foster a thriving social scene. For much of Europe's history, this place was the local pub. But for the Turkish in the Ottoman Empire, it was the local coffee house, as most people in this empire followed the Islamic faith. "Thus, alcoholic consumption was taboo, making the growth of coffee houses a perfect location for individuals to gather and discuss their ideas with others. Coffee houses became the primary social scene for the Ottomans to meet with others. Discussing politics, business, or voicing an opinion were frowned upon in mosques" (Rosenberg, 1). Imagine the meeting of minds, the whisper of descent in these humble tiny coffee houses, wide and far; this would be an Achilles heel for Sultans for centuries to come.

What was so revolutionary about these coffee houses was that people from every social standing could sit together and be equals. Coffee houses were not exclusive to the town's elites.

They were welcoming places for those from the highest and lowest tiers of society to come together and discuss their world. However, women were still excluded from these coffee houses. All conversations held within were for men's ears only. Despite excluding half of the population, the humble coffee houses became dens for philosophy and revolution. Before this point in history, there was nothing. Never had there been a place where people could sit as equals to enjoy a drink, crossing a cultural and societal void. As more people could voice their opinions to others, social hierarchies became diluted with loose lips and whispers of unrest; these were dangerous times for the sultans. Never before could an idea spread amongst the population at such an alarming speed; the sultans had every right to be worried.

The social unrest in the humble coffee houses caused the sultans to act against them and the drink itself. Several times throughout the Ottoman Empire's history, coffee was banned by sultans trying to subdue social uprisings, rebellion, and their possible demise. The ideas spreading within coffee houses were dangerous, leading to people wanting more freedom from their rulers. In response, the coffee houses were closed to 'fix' the conflict. "In 1663, Sultan Murad IV had a personal vendetta and decided that drinking coffee was a capital offense, and personally hunted down offenders to decapitate them with his broadsword. Murad's brother and uncle had been killed by infantry units known to visit coffee houses" (Rotondi, 1) and decided that drinking coffee was criminal activity.

Despite the pushback, coffee houses still thrived. But instead of being open on the streets, they became hidden in back alleys away from the prying eyes of palace spies. Coffee drinking never died due to the decrees, and the banning of coffee often led to pushback, forcing the sultans to make it legal again. This cycle of appreciation, banning, and resurgence happened many times throughout the Ottoman Empire. Coffee houses had a way of persisting through the thick and thin of social disputes. The value they contributed to people was too great and would not be gone forever. But the influence of coffee houses did not end there. As coffee traveled around the world, it soon found its hold in Europe, where coffee houses repeated history, finding more love from their fellow Europeans and resistance from their leaders.

European Coffee Houses

For many years, coffee didn't reach other parts of the world. The Ottomans treasured the plant too much to let others take it, so they attempted to monopolize the trade from the west. But eventually, coffee made its way north and took hold in Germany and England, where coffee houses like the Ottomans began to pop up. They soon took hold of the social nature of discussion much as they did in the Ottoman Empire and even faced the same backlash from rulers. Still, the drink persisted throughout Europe. Coffee houses held a prominent place for discussions on revolution and social change amidst the scientific and industrial revolution.

Coffee began to take hold in Europe roughly four hundred years after it started in the Ottoman Empire. After trade routes had become well-established worldwide, it was much easier to bring coffee beans north. English coffee houses were particularly prevalent in the 1700s because their atmosphere served a similar purpose to the Ottoman coffee houses. "According to some records, the first English coffee house was brought over from Turkey by a Greek-Orthodox servant named Pasqua

Rosee" (Suter, 107). Englishmen found the effects of the drink delightful and perfect for stimulating conversation. But the coffee houses themselves are why coffee was so successful in this part of the world. Unlike Islamic practices, which were most common for people to practice in the middle eastern part of the world, Christian Protestantism did not require long hours of religious practices. So there was less of a practical need for coffee as people did not need to stay up through long nights for religious ceremonies. But the accessibility of these coffee houses was able to draw people from all social classes together in one room in a more respectable manner than a tap house. "The drink was also cheaper and healthier for people and worked against the avid drunkenness that often polluted the streets of London" (Suter, 107).

Restaurants and eateries spent a lot of money and time specializing in creating and serving meals - unlike coffee houses, which were able to reduce this by limiting their menu to varieties of a drink, which made prices for dining lower than other shops. "Because of this affordability, the middle-class could participate in coffee enjoyment, usually reserved for the social elite" (Ramjattan, 1). England had a strict hierarchy, and the idea of people of different standings sitting together was revolutionary for the time. Much like the story of the Ottomans, this allowed conversations between people to flourish. Whether or not this new atmosphere created the intellectual movement or fostered it, coffee houses arose at the perfect time to contribute to the Age of Enlightenment. A time when the exchanging of ideas and philosophies allowed the world to collectively grow its social mind and brew ideas to make a better future.

Coffee houses were frequented specifically by politically-minded people, who would not be able to voice their opinions in a pub to risk a dangerous conflict. "There was an iconic setup to the English coffee house. Large communal tables filled with pamphlets and papers of all subjects, with men surrounding the tables consuming, discussing, and writing news" (Ramjattan, 1). "English coffee houses were soon named penny universities, as one without much education would be able to sit among scholars and learn through participating in their discussions" (Rotondi, 1). "There were, of course, only men permitted in coffee houses; they did not accept women" (Suter, 107). "However, women were able to run and operate the businesses, with a 'coffee woman' often running the business, ensuring it was an enjoyable place to visit" (Suter, 108). Although women could be in the building, it was not acceptable for them to sit and have discussions.

Because lower class people were allowed in coffee houses, those of the higher classes tended to stay away from them to avoid losing their reputation. But with the discussion of politics and change, those who benefited from the current model became frightened by the ideas that emerged. King Charles II was particularly paranoid about the effects of coffee and coffee houses on his reign; his father was decapitated during the civil war. In 1672, "Charles decided to prohibit coffee consumption" (Rotondi, 1) by making a proclamation, "To Restrain the Spreading of False News, and Licentious Talking of Matters of State and Government," (Rotondi, 1), which detailed how "men have assumed to themselves a liberty, not only in coffee houses but in other places and meetings, both public and private, to censure and defame the proceedings of State by speaking evil of things they understand not" (Rotondi, 1). He was so serious about this decree, he sent state spies to infiltrate coffee houses and arrest the offenders. In December 1675, Charles forced the closure of coffee houses, but in light of a people's revolt eleven days later, he was forced to reopen the coffee house.

King Charles II was not the only European monarch to find coffee an evil drink. King Frederick, the Great of Germany, despised coffee because of his business interest in beer consumption. "In 1777, he banned his people from drinking coffee and forced coffee houses to register with the state for a license" (Rotoni,1). Frederick allowed his personal friends permittance, making it a drink only for the aristocracy. As he pushed this campaign against coffee, he tried to convince his people that beer was better for them. "Frederic stated that he and many soldiers had won wars by drinking beer, the only drink people needed" (Brooks, 1). Although his hatred for coffee seems passionate, historians associate it with coffee's economic worries for the country. Frederick was worried that money was flowing out of the country with coffee purchases, so the government needed to switch to beer to bring it back. But the reason for this is likely similar to that of King Charles' situation; the whispers of social unrest that could spread rapidly within coffee houses were dangerous for his position.

Despite the pushback from European leaders, coffee houses began popping up all over the continent. The English, German, French, and Italian loved the drink; they evolved separately in each country with their unique style. The Italian espresso and the French press are just a few examples of how Europeans adopted this African product for themselves and created social powerhouses with it. The coffee house allowed people of all social standings to come together, learn, and discuss politics, science, and culture. We cannot say how many ideas were born in these coffee houses that affect our lives today, but there is no denying Europeans' love of coffee and the social interaction within the walls of the humble coffee house.

Modern Day Coffee Houses

If your interest in coffee has progressed thus far, you are likely familiar with the atmosphere and culture that surrounds it. For some, the draw comes from the calming environment with the aromatic scent of fresh coffee beans in the air. For others, it is the casual ability to meet up with old friends or enjoy open mic poetry nights. Coffee houses act as a unique place for every person who visits them. Even after the American revolution, coffee houses did not die out when there was no political need. Instead, the world transformed them into places meant to enjoy culture and history as people perfected their craft of coffee making.

Cultures worldwide have claimed coffee as their own, inventing new and better ways to consume it. Coffee shops have become famous landmarks in cities across Europe for their exceptional craft of coffee and the significance of its purpose in the culture. For example, Café de la Paix is notably the most famous coffee house in France. "Created in the late 1800s, it stood as a meeting location for many prominent intellectuals, politicians, and artists, and was even a showcase for developing films" (Smith, 1). Even in modern times, coffee houses remain places for people to gather and experience the fascinations of our society and world together. Italians are known for their love of enjoying their espresso in cafes, which is why it is often referred to as the world's coffee capital. Italy is full of coffee houses established decades ago that have worked hard to make the best coffee available. The culture has deep roots, so they are reluctant to allow the megacorporation Starbucks into their country, gatekeeping their coffee from becoming Americanized.

The coffee houses that most may be familiar with are not historical and bare no cultural significance, yet they are the prominent brands found in every city. Starbucks and Dunkin Donuts are among the most significant coffee companies globally and provide a large majority of coffee houses. Although loved by many, these brands show a dilution of coffee culture. The success of coffee has ultimately led to the big brand and, in a small part, the death of the coffee-making craft. Even though they are the most common coffee houses found worldwide, there is still room for artisanal coffee shops to thrive.

Because of coffee's popularity and the current globalization of the trade, modern coffee houses allow people from non-coffee growing regions to enjoy quality coffee grown from different cultures; no matter which cafe you walk into, you can find coffee grown in several areas. Depending on your preferred level of roast, enjoying the various coffee flavors is on a similar level of diversity as wine or beer, making it an integral part of daily life and an opportunity to grow preferences. The sheer size of coffee variety and production are impressive and have changed dramatically over the centuries. Still, our personal and social connection to the drink remains the same, regardless of time, culture, and location. And it all pulls back to the historical significance and impact coffee houses have had on our world.

There are many reasons why coffee houses are so successful. One could factor in the atmosphere, functionality, and economic profitability to explain the necessity of coffee. But there seems to be a vibrant relationship between humanity and coffee. Beyond the factual appearance of the industry, it seems to call on our sense of community and collective enjoyment of the drink. It's almost as if the coffee itself is only a tiny part of why we love the coffee house. It ultimately comes from the centuries when coffee houses interacted as facilitators for societies with a deep appreciation for a great cup of coffee.

CHAPTER 2

COFFEE AND POLYPHENOL

"Live long and prosper"

People tend to indulge in food and drinks that are deliciously decadent but may not be that healthy for our bodies; luckily for humanity, coffee is not one of these indulgences! Health benefits are abundant in drinking coffee and many parts of the coffee bean. Coffee includes polyphenols, antioxidants, and various other properties that are valuable to our health in a multitude of aspects. However, too much of a good thing can be harmful! Coffee is proven to help with some skin issues and improve the microcirculation within layers of skin. Evidence suggests that coffee can help with weight loss and metabolic problems, and even help your brain function. Yet, coffee has some drawbacks, such as its effect on the cardiovascular system. Still, many scientists agree that coffee is good for you when moderately consumed! Most of these benefits come from the polyphenols held within coffee beans, so let us examine this compound and how your daily cup of coffee can benefit you long past the caffeine wake-up call.

What is Polyphenol?

Polyphenol is a broadly encompassing term for many active elements in our food. "Polyphenols are plant compounds that offer various health benefits" (Petre, 1). These compounds can work across your whole body; you can find many in your daily coffee fix. They act like antioxidants and neutralize agents that might otherwise cause harm to your cells. Coffee can have so many benefits, from helping your skin to assisting in cancer prevention. "Studies have shown that coffee is one of the biggest suppliers of antioxidants in our diet" (Bajarnadottir, 1). Not all polyphenols are equal; their presence in your coffee depends on the variety of the bean, harvest, transportation, and how long they have been sitting on your shelf.

In the same way that each cup of coffee is unique, the amount of these beneficial compounds varies depending on the coffee itself. A study conducted by the European Food Research and Technology group found that polyphenol levels rely on coffee's cultivation, roast, and storage. "The first to cover is the cultivation method of the beans; they discovered that organically-grown beans contain significantly higher amounts of polyphenols than conventional beans" (Krol, 36). The difference between these two growing methods is that, after storing the beans for 12 months, the organic beans held the polyphenol compounds much better. "The roast level of the beans also had a significant effect, as lightly roasted coffee retained the antioxidant properties and caffeine much better than the dark roast" (Krol, 38). This finding is logical since polyphenols are plant-based compounds and are heat-sensitive; the longer the roast, the lower the component. Polyphenols deteriorate with age. So, if you would like the best health effects from your coffee, choose fresh, organic, light roast coffee!

Polyphenols and Metabolism

Weight gain issues concern people for aesthetic and medical purposes, but coffee polyphenols are there to help. The evidence for the idea that coffee helps with metabolism is still ongoing but is providing promising results as an effective way to treat weight gain. "A study in Japan experimented with coffee polyphenols and weight accumulation with mice and found that those given the coffee supplement alongside a high-fat diet retained less fat than those not given the coffee" (Murase, 125). The study concluded that coffee polyphenols enhance energy metabolism and kickstart our system, "which leads to the suppression of body fat accumulation" (Murase, 125). Coffee is a stimulant; it excites your nervous system in different ways.

One form of this excitement is through an energy boost, but your body's different facets feel this too. Caffeine tells your nervous system to get excited; "it sends out epinephrine doses, also known as adrenaline" (Gunnars, 1). This hormone goes through your body, letting it know that it is ready to go and should burn some energy. Your fat cells begin to break down to feed whatever activity it thinks is coming. The polyphenols follow this process and help where they can.

Not only can coffee contribute to helping to burn fat as you drink, but it also works to increase your resting metabolic rate. "Your metabolic rate is when you burn fat without moving; those with higher rates can lose weight quickly" (Gunnars, 1). "Studies have found that drinking coffee can increase your resting metabolic rate from three to eleven percent, depending on the dosage of caffeine" (Gunnars, 1). "Coffee is not the solution to weight loss, as these effects have shown to be more effective in people who are already lean rather than obese" (Gunnars, 1). The benefit seems to also decrease with age as well as tolerance. Any avid coffee drinker knows the more coffee you drink, the lighter the buzz will be; this is due to our tolerance levels increasing with time as you feel the energy spike less and less, meaning your metabolism and fat-burning signals are not as strong as when you first began drinking coffee. Unfortunately, it is not a perfect solution to all metabolic problems. It works best within young, lean people and decreases with tolerance over time. Although coffee is not the golden ticket to weight loss, coffee's various polyphenols and caffeine levels are still helpful for your mind and body.

Polyphenols and Skin Health

The skin is the largest and most visible organ, and many people are interested in keeping it healthy and beautiful. Studies have shown several benefits for your epidermis from ingesting coffee and have shown that coffee can help your skin retain water and fight against internal damages, such as dryness. Polyphenols activate signaling proteins to eliminate senescent cells within our bodies. Our skin is our first line of defense and is the only organ exposed to the elements daily. Bacteria and other pathogens are constantly attacking our skin. We tend to overlook skin health as vanity; however, what's on the outside indicates our general health and biological age; if you are old on the outside, you are old on the inside. Widespread agitations like dry patches, pimples, or wrinkles may seem ordinary but are signs of an unhealthy organ. One of the best ways to help this is to make sure your skin retains water, allowing blood to circulate through your skin more efficiently, strengthening your skin's natural barrier. Studies have shown that polyphenols in coffee are beneficial to the skin's health!

Another benefit of coffee is its effect on the pH level of your skin. "The pH of the surface of your skin increases with age, and higher pH levels lead to issues such as atopic dermatitis and xerosis" (Fukagawa, 1818). These can arise from a dysfunctional skin barrier. Studies have shown that coffee can help lower your skin's pH. A recent study showed that drinking three cups of coffee a day has anti-aging effects. The study that concluded these findings used organic green coffee beans as their source for the polyphenols; organic coffee is better for your health in many ways. These benefits are through oral consumption of coffee but also topical applicants. Even if you do not want to buy new creams with coffee polyphenols, you can still receive these benefits by drinking moderate coffee daily. Drinking organic coffee will not wholly cure that persistent rash or make skin look younger overnight. Still, it is a step toward healthy living. As you sip on your favorite tiple at your favorite cafe, rest assured that the polyphenols will be working to strengthen your skin and help prevent future problems. Go on, do a Benjamin Button and grow just that little bit younger. Polyphenols and Brain Health.

Polyphenols and Brain Health

Healthy cognitive function is essential for many aspects of our health; "studies have shown coffee to help significantly prevent conditions like Alzheimer's" (Ishida, 35). As mentioned before, the polyphenols in coffee work in many ways, disabling processes in our body that damage cells. This damage leads to our brains losing function and developing more severe diseases. When people call coffee their 'brain juice,' they are not entirely wrong! The benefits of coffee work on two different fronts, preventing damage to brain cells and restoration. To better understand, let us look at them separately. Antioxidants work within our body depending on the needs and role of our organs. Our brains have the lowest level of antioxidant activity in our body; this deterioration leads to loss of cognitive function and the development of diseases in the brain. Therefore, the antioxidants in coffee benefit our brain by preventing this breakdown of our neurons. Scientists are unsure if these have the power to entirely prevent neurological diseases such as Parkinson's or Alzheimer's disease. Still, as the research develops, it is already clear that good coffee can help increase and preserve your brain function. Having a cup or two of coffee a day can help your brain stay healthy for longer than if you did not get that extra intake of antioxidant polyphenols.

The antioxidant packed-polyphenols in coffee can cross the blood-brain barrier, helping with memory and the ability to problem-solve. The results from studies on coffee's effects differ, so nothing is known for sure, but recently, one study found "that the consistent intake of coffee over a four to six-month period improved cognitive function in the elderly" (Ishida, 36). Other studies found that recognition enhanced with the input of coffee polyphenols improved performance on memory tests. These findings also suggested an improvement in motivation and motor function. They indicate that coffee can improve your mood, memory, movement, and overall brain function by clearing up the metaphorical gunk that slows down your brain to help your brain stay healthy. Although there is emerging evidence that coffee can help slow Alzheimer's, more clinical studies are needed. A study done by biology scientists in Japan showed that coffee could help treat one of the contributors to the development of Alzheimer's. Even though there have been no trials or studies on Alzheimer's patients, it is encouraging to see how coffee can help the brain function in people of all ages and may lead to finding a cure.

Polyphenols and Disease

If these reasons were not enough to convince you of the power of coffee polyphenols, studies have shown that these polyphenols can help prevent diseases such as cancers and diabetes. "The active compounds in coffee take part in various biological processes, as they exhibit chemoprotective effects, antioxidant and anti-inflammatory properties, and anticancer activity" (LIczbiński, 2). Drinking coffee can protect against cardiovascular disease, obesity, some types of cancer, and type 2 diabetes. "A Danish study found that drinking three to four cups of coffee a day could help prevent the development of

Parkinson's and Type 2 Diabetes" (Hermansen, 1). The possible diabetes treatment is interesting because of how the polyphenols interact with the body's sugar regulation; coffee polyphenols activate the AMPK pathway and down-regulate mTOR and insulin pathways. These polyphenols assist the pancreas in delaying the increase in glucose levels in the blood, stabilizing blood sugar, thereby preventing the development of diabetes. Those at risk of diabetes may find that a coffee or three a day may slow the onset of diabetes due to the natural polyphenols.

Cancers are another set of diseases that plague our society. Cancer forms when dysfunctional senescent cells mutate and multiply out of control. Senescent mutated cells come from malfunctions in our cell's mitosis system; this alone does not form malignant cancer, as our body has mechanisms to prevent those cells from becoming a problem. But when those systems stop working, cancer finds its hold. Polyphenols help keep our systems healthy and can therefore help in preventing cancer. Emerging evidence shows that coffee polyphenols help slow or prevent some cancers, "including head and neck, colorectal, breast, and liver cancer" (Mendes, 1). Although the types of cancers coffee can prevent are highly debated, scientists agree that polyphenols have a role in the future of health. Polyphenols in coffee beans "have been shown to increase energy expenditure, inhibit cellular damage, regulate genes involved in DNA repair, have anti-inflammatory properties, and inhibit metastasis" (Mendes, 1); these help your body prevent cancerous cells from growing out of control! Scientists can hopefully improve ways to utilize polyphenols with more research, but for now, you can give yourself an extra boost of protection from some daily cups of coffee. Conclusion.

Conclusion

One thing to note about these benefits is how different varieties of coffee have varying effects on our bodies. Organic light roasted coffee is the best way to get the health benefits from your drink, keeping in mind that some coffee can do more harm than good for you. "Aluminum is a very toxic element in our body linked to many human deaths and the development of cancers" (LIczbiński, 5). "As it turns out, decaffeinated and instant coffee significantly contribute to how aluminum gets into our bodies" (LIczbiński, 5). It is essential to understand that not all coffee is created equal, and the benefits discovered come from quality organic coffee; inferior coffees have minimum health benefits.

Excluding the toxic element of decaffeinated coffee, coffee is being researched more and more as a healthy contributor to our well-being. It can help keep us from getting sick in more ways than one and even reverse some health issues - all thanks to the polyphenols in coffee. Of course, coffee is not our holy grail to end everything that ails us. It is highly variable from how the coffee is grown, roasted, stored, and brewed, on top of how each person will take in different levels of effects. It is not perfect, but you can still rely on how your coffee is not a harmful and indulgent contribution to your body. Instead, it can keep you active and healthy for longer. So, continue indulging, to quote Spock from Star Trek, *"live long and prosper"*.

COFFEE

CHAPTER 3

WORLD ATLAS COFFEE

"Charming coffee with nutty tones"

Coffee originated in Africa but has since spread worldwide for consumption and production. With the demand for coffee being so high, there has been space for the coffee tree to thrive in regions worldwide. Like other plant-based beverages, beer, wine, and tea, the natural climate, and earth the coffee tree

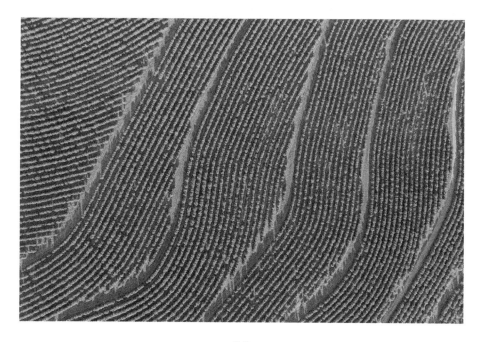

grows in introduces a unique complex of flavors. Allowing for coffee with different degrees of flavor and texture to be readily available and is marked with pride by the country of origin.

Although the coffee plant may not be native to many of the world's highest-producing coffee regions, people have adopted it as their own and delight in making beans desirable worldwide. Whether you frequent your local Starbucks or an artisanal shop, you have probably seen options for coffee from Colombia, Brazil, Guatemala, Ethiopia, Vietnam, and many others. Coffee trees can be particular about where they like to grow, but if you find the right conditions, they can thrive and grow with a unique flavor profile you cannot find anywhere else.

This atlas of coffee-growing regions is called the 'coffee belt.' The best conditions for growing coffee are rich, warm, and wet forests that lie between the Tropics of Cancer and Capricorn. These regions are around the Earth's equator, creating this belt of coffee that wraps around the globe. Each location produces various amounts and types of coffee, all with different practices for planting, growing, harvesting, and processing the precious coffee bean. We will review what makes each region in the world's atlas of coffee unique and show how not all coffee is created equal.

Central America Coffee

Central America is among one of the top-rated coffee-growing regions in the world. The tall mountains, temperate climate, and rich volcanic soil all collaborate to make some of the best coffee you can find. All Central American countries produce coffee for export within the coffee belt. Each country has its flavor profile, growing seasons, and specified amount of coffee produced each year from southern Mexico to Panama. Since it is so closely accessible to the United States, much of the coffee you have consumed in your life has likely originated in this region. So let us examine some of the countries that produce the best quality coffee globally.

Costa Rica draws in money from tourism and coffee sales. People travel to Costa Rica to enjoy the beaches, jungle, and superb coffee, with tours of coffee plantations being a popular activity. Costa Rica is full of well-drained volcanic soil, which has helped make its coffee full-bodied and packed with rich chocolatey notes. Coffee arrived in Costa Rica around 1729 and has since become one of its most significant exports, "bringing in 25% of the country's earnings. Roughly 1,700kg per hectare of coffee produced by 400 million coffee trees" (Pebble & Pine,1). "Some of the best coffee found in the world comes from Tarrazu" (Pebble & Pine,1), as it has a clean flavor and intoxicating fragrance. Until recently, Costa Rica had banned the production of coffee from Robusta beans, choosing only to grow Arabica coffee beans. Robusta beans contain more caffeine, but Arabica coffee is often smoother and sweeter. Costa Rica made Robusta production illegal to promote Arabica beans. But with the rise in temperatures within the country, "Costa Rican leaders are deeply considering removing this ban because Robusta beans grow better in hotter climates" (Reini, 1).

Guatemala is another country in Central America known for its impeccable coffee. Guatemala is uniquely located among tectonic plates, resulting in large amounts of volcanic activity. "Which is great for its coffee, as the ash from these eruptions settles into the soil and adds extra nutrients like nitrogen which helps create very balanced coffee" (Pebble & Pine, 1). Guatemalan coffee tends to be medium in body and acidity with gentle berry, citrus, and vanilla notes. Unfortunately, this incredible coffee is threatened by a devastating fungus that grows on the leaves of coffee trees and prevents them from collecting and processing the sunlight they need. The Rust, or la Roya in Spanish, was brought from South Asia and ran rampant throughout Central and South America. "The Rust has reached the majority of coffee crops in this region, hitting Guatemala particularly hard with nearly 70% of coffee trees infected" (Khan, 1). It gets worse as the fungus is a fan of hot climates. As temperatures rise, it can thrive at higher altitudes than before. And since the best coffee is grown at these altitudes, coffee production is rapidly decreasing. There is research to help find variants resistant to rust, but it remains a severe problem for coffee growers and drinkers alike.

South American Coffee

Due to South America's large amounts of rainforests, it is one of the perfect places for coffee production. Central America's soil is rich in nutrients due to the heavy volcanic activity depositing sentiments around the region. But, South America benefits in the same way from many centuries of humidity and plant growth. As plants and animals die, they replenish the soil with all the necessary nutrients, perfect for more organisms to take their place. It gives South American coffee a deep flavor profile and a great growing space. This region creates the most coffee on the planet and is favored by large companies and artisanal coffee shops worldwide. South American coffee is generally medium-bodied, smooth, and easy to drink. "The unique soil it grows on leads it to often have chocolatey, nutty, spicy flavors" (Neighborhood, 1). Coffee is grown in many South American countries, such as Peru, Brazil, Colombia, Venezuela, etc. With fewer topographical differences in the landscape than in Central America's many mountains, it is easier to produce large amounts of coffee. Coffee production here does lead to large amounts of deforestation, as farmers clear-cut rainforests to make room for their crops. Despite the various problems this causes, South America still produces large quantities of the most outstanding coffee in the world for everyone to enjoy.

Brazil is the largest coffee producer in the entire world! "Roughly 29% of the whole world's coffee production comes from just one country" (Neighborhood, 1), and it makes sense seeing as they have so much space to do so. "Brazil exports roughly 2.6 million metric tons of coffee each year, where it has been the leader in coffee distribution volume for one hundred and fifty years" (Neighborhood, 1). Like many other Central and South American coffees, Brazil primarily works with Arabica coffee beans growing them in regions about four thousand to six thousand feet above sea level. The warm, humid temperatures mixed with the rich soil create a mild coffee flavor with chocolate, nuttiness, and caramel notes. These attributes are why people love Brazilian coffee, as it is easier to drink and naturally sweeter than coffee from other parts of the world. Because of the sheer amount exported, it is probably one of the most accessible types of coffee you can find no matter where you live. "Brazil's states of Minas Gerais, São Paulo, and Paraná are the largest producers of coffee as they come with the perfect climate and elevation" (Blue Coffee Box, 1). Brazilians also tend to harvest these coffee beans between May and July in the dry season.

Colombia is another of the largest coffee producers globally, but it is distinctly different from neighboring countries. Most of their coffee is grown in the three long mountain ranges. Coffee production is successful due to the small microclimates pocketed along the mountain ranges. Unlike Brazil, where extensive plantations are maintained, Colombia is full of many smaller plantations. Because each microclimate creates different conditions, the coffee on each farm is ready at different times of the year, which is pretty unique! The flavor profile of this coffee is similar to Brazil's but with more floral notes and a higher level of acidity. If you see Colombian coffee at the supermarket, you may notice terms like Supremo or Excelso on the packaging, which refers to the size and quality of the coffee bean! Although each region uses its own coffee bean grading system, Colombia is the only one to use these words to describe its coffee. "Supremo describes the larger and higher-quality beans, while Excelso labels the medium-to-small ones" (Ospina, 1). As the third-largest coffee producer globally, Colombian coffee is a favorite among many; a high-quality option for your daily caffeine needs.

Peruvian coffee offers another unique combination of flavors to South American coffee. "Grown in the high mountains of the Andes, Peruvian coffee is grown on small farms less than two hectares in size" (Blue Coffee Box, 1)! These farms are spread throughout the country and produce a lighter coffee than their neighbors with a long bright finish. Peruvian coffee has many obstacles in its production. First is the weather phenomenon of El Nino, an event that results in dry arid periods for a year; this results in poor growing conditions and a lower yield. Coffee grows best in the equatorial region because of the constant rainfall. There is also trouble with the distribution of the coffee. Peru has many tall mountains and deep valleys, making transportation very difficult. Due to such harsh terrain, resources are often limited; this can be magnified in an El Nino event, making it challenging to get help. The coffee, however, is delicious and often organic! "Peru has many requirements preventing the spraying of coffee plantations with pesticides, synthetic fertilizers, or chemicals that can leak into the bean" (Blue Coffee Box). Peru is the third-highest producer of coffee in South America, and its unique taste and history make these beans stand out among the rest.

Middle Eastern Coffee

Coffee houses may have originated in the Middle East, but recently, they have not been a popular region to grow coffee. The hot, dry weather makes it much more difficult to grow coffee trees than in the lush forests of Latin America. Yet, it is still one of the original homes of the coffee drink, and therefore the locals grow and drink it daily. "The coffee drink symbolizes respect in the Middle East, as people consider it rude not to accept coffee offered to you when you are meeting someone" (Khan, 2020). Most of the coffee produced in the Middle East came from Yemen until recently. "The Saudi Arabian government has been pushing to encourage the coffee market and has since seen sales skyrocket" (Tark, 1). This surge in coffee has had some interesting effects on Saudi culture! Recently, the government has loosened social laws that now "allow men and women together in some social spaces like coffee houses" (Khan, 2020). These changes have again fostered social movements, as the coffee houses are becoming places of social change. Depending on how the politics of Arabian coffee develop, we may be seeing more Middle Eastern coffee on the shelves in supermarkets.

Yemen was the most well-known coffee producer in the Middle East before it was closed off. "Coffee from Yemen must be grown in dry, arid climates, making the resulting beans smaller and more irregular than others" (NCA, 1). Due to this climate, the coffee beans are all sun-dried, as this process is the best way to preserve all the flavor in the beans before roasting them. These arid combinations make the coffee from this region rich with an incredibly distinct chocolatey flavor. Coffee from Yemen is often called 'Yemen Mocha' beans, named after a famous coffee trading port. At one point, the Dutch traders bought some of these beans and blended them with beans from the island of Java. This created the first coffee blend still recognizable today, the Mocha Java. Coffee from this region also tends to be very full-bodied, with high acidity and spiced notes included. It is prevalent for Middle Eastern people to drink their coffee with cardamom, so it can often be found as a subtle flavor in the beans. Middle Eastern coffee is not a region that comes to mind when people consider where the best coffee in the world comes from? But as time goes on, it will hopefully resurge and be able to share its historic coffee beans with the world again.

African Coffee

As the origin of the coffee tree itself, Africa is home to some of the world's most decadent coffee. Coffee is produced all around this vast continent, but only a few countries produce most African coffee. "These are Ethiopia, Uganda, and Kenya, which produce two-thirds of the continent's coffee" (Mungai, 1). Unlike the coffee regions previously covered, "African people do not consume coffee the same way; it is primarily an exportation crop" (Mungai,1). Many Africans prefer tea to coffee, which is interesting when noticing that coffee originated there! "Some of the best African coffee comes from plantations along the banks of the African Great Lakes, where cool climates, rich soil, and plenty of rainfall make for excellent coffee beans" (Felongco, 1). The flavors in African coffee are often distinct, with lots of fruity and floral notes and well-balanced acidity and mouthfeel.

Ethiopia is often a favorite among coffee drinkers due to the volcanic soil creating rich flavors different from those in Central America. This coffee tends to be very fruity and winey in taste, further retained through its drying process. Coffee trees produce coffee cherries containing the coffee bean inside. Once the fruit has ripened, there are two ways to extract the bean - dry the berries in the sun or wash the berry away from the bean. African countries tend to use both of these methods, depending on the weather, as water scarcity or heavy rainfall can prevent either technique. Most people agree that sun drying the berries is the best method to use overall as it keeps the flavor locked inside the bean, which is why Ethiopian coffee can taste so fruity. Although, washing the beans can take some of the sharpness out of the coffee, making it sweeter and gentler to enjoy. Unlike other African countries, Ethiopia has been producing coffee for centuries, whereas other African countries have only started coffee production in the last hundred years. "They have perfected the process and are the fifth-highest coffee producer globally" (Felongco, 1), and their unique flavors set them apart from many other coffees.

Uganda is another one of the highest coffee-producing countries in Africa, and not only grows a unique variety but processes them differently, too. The majority of regions and countries covered so far produce "Arabica coffee beans, as they are of higher quality and grow well in high altitudes. Uganda uses almost 80% Robusta" (Espresso and Coffee Guide, Uganda), making their coffee milder and sweeter. Ugandan coffee is usually smooth-bodied with a winey acidity and full of fruity notes such as orange and pineapple. The coffee is also mostly washed instead of dried, so it is sweet and easy to drink. "Coffee grown around Lake Victoria is a special blend of Robusta beans grown in cooler high-altitude climates" (Espresso and Coffee Guide, Uganda). This allows for more acidity than beans grown in lower elevations, resulting in the best blend of both worlds for coffee flavors.

Do you like coffee with fruity flavors but still want a deep and rich cup of joe? Kenya offers this perfect balance for coffee connoisseurs. "Kenya is known to have one of the top five best coffees globally" (Espresso and Coffee Guide, Kenya). The coffee beans from this country tend to be high in acidity and have a more full-bodied taste while retaining the floral aroma typical to the neighboring countries. The after-taste of Kenyan coffee can be distinct, often dry with a lemony flavor. Overall, you can expect this coffee to be fruity, well-balanced, and rich. Kenya has the most consistent high-quality coffee beans available as they are highly renowned in the coffee community. They have also made the coffee distribution process quick and easy, so the beans do not wait too long to be sold or roasted.

Southeast Asian Coffee

Other coffee-producing regions often overshadow southeast Asia, but it does not mean their coffee is worse. "This may have come from the fact that Asia produces a lot of the cheap coffee used for instant mixes and other low-quality products" (Espresso International, 1). But there are plenty of countries that produce high-quality coffee, which is just as unique and tasty as anywhere else! China, India, Thailand, Vietnam, and Indonesia are just a few of the big producers in Asia. Southeast Asia is particularly suited for coffee growing, so the best coffees usually come from Vietnam and Indonesia. We will look deeper into these countries, but Southeast Asian coffee has an overall exotic flavor profile. It is often dark and full-bodied, with low acidity and nutty or spicy undertones. "This coffee is described as creamy and smooth, but with a moderate-to-heavy mouthfeel" (Queen Bean, 2018). There is much to discover with this region's coffee, so let us look at the notable coffee stars who shine!

"Vietnam is the world's second-highest producer of coffee, just behind Brazil" (Espresso International, 1) - this is crazy if you consider the vast differences in land quantity between the two countries! "Vietnam mainly produces the Robusta bean, with this variety taking over 90% of the country's coffee production" (Espresso International, 1). These coffee beans are high in acidity, with chocolatey and caramel notes complimenting a medium-dark roast perfectly. Because of the high acidity and sweet flavors, there is a certain way to drink coffee in Vietnam: placing the ground Robusta beans in a cup and add hot water, sugar, and sweet condensed milk. You drink it just like that, grinds and all! Although you aren't required to drink Vietnamese coffee this way, the charming coffee with nutty tones is excellent for brewing methods and perfect for introducing yourself to all the varieties of coffee.

Although Thailand may not be one of the biggest producers of coffee in Southeast Asia, its relationship with coffee throughout its history has been exciting and noteworthy. Thailand is new to the coffee game as production began in the 1970s. Many small farmers had opium fields that provided income while unfortunately providing the world with a drug problem. To stop this, "the Thai government began encouraging farmers to switch their crops to Arabica coffee" (Espresso International, 1). These efforts were considerate of the environment, as they chose not to clear-cut the forests to plant coffee trees. "Instead, they cleared out the undergrowth and planted them below a light canopy" (Espresso International, 1). This improves the quality of the coffee, protecting them from weather and disease, as coffee trees do not thrive in direct sunlight. These efforts helped create the Doi Chaing coffee variety, which is rated one of the best in the world. This coffee is often light in its acidity, with savory notes from the trees growing around it: nutty, spicy, full-flavored, and creamy mark Thai coffee is an incredibly masterful composition. Since then, coffee production and culture in this region have grown immensely, particularly in the northern region around Chiang Mai, where coffee houses can be found in abundance.

No coffee is created equal; each farm will make coffee with different flavors, and each country will provide different soils that will change the way the coffee bean develops. There is no way to determine which country or region creates the best coffee because the enjoyment of coffee is not entirely measurable. It depends on different tastes, preferences, and histories with the drink. Those who have tasted every coffee in the world can choose their favorite cup; however, this is different for each individual. This is why coffee lovers adore trying exceptional coffee from around the world. Because maybe that small brand that grows coffee on a mountainside in Guatemala is the perfect coffee for you; you just have to find it.

CHAPTER 4

BUYING COFFEE

"What makes your tongue dance"

This may come as no shock, but coffee is all about its taste. Buying good coffee is not necessarily about finding the best beans in the entire world because opinions vary based on what makes your tongue dance. The beauty of coffee is exploring which elements you prefer and determining which variety soothes your soul the best. It takes some trial and error, but the ultimate goal is to find which balance of acidity, flavors, and body you prefer. There is fun in the experience, yet even with experimentation, it is good to know where to start. There are so many different brands to choose from that it can be overwhelming, and understanding some basic tenants of coffee can help start you on your journey.

Buying good coffee is best when you know what you are looking for; wandering aimlessly down the grocery aisles will get you drinkable coffee, but unless you know what flavors or varieties you prefer and understand how the beans reached you, it can be tricky to find coffee of a higher caliber. This chapter will review the various aspects of coffee to consider as you shop, and some items to look out for to help determine which beans are best. The coffee world is ever-growing in popularity, and it may feel overwhelming. As long as you can establish what all the numbers mean on the packaging and which numbers you know you like, you can quickly move forward and pick out the best coffee.

We have already established the basic flavor principles of coffee, such as acidity and mouthfeel. These are good to keep in mind as you hunt for good coffee because they can guide you in the right direction. But understanding a few more dimensions of coffee, such as how it matches your preferred brewing method, is even more helpful to narrow down the search. There are many badges or stickers you might see on coffee bags. Frankly, there are numerous grading and certification systems in place, but we will review the most important ones to help you further determine the perfect coffee. Finally, once you have a better grasp on what beans are suitable for you, we will examine

some purchasing methods that do not include simply picking one off the shelf at your grocery store.

Dimensions of Coffee

By now, you should have a good understanding of how each coffee bag is different from the next based on its region, drying process, and variety. There are still more dimensions to coffee that are helpful to know when looking to buy quality. You may often see the flavor notes associated with different coffee-growing regions. To generalize, chocolatey notes come from Central and South America, fruity notes come from Africa, and caramelly nutty notes from Southeast Asia. Of course, you can still find all flavor profiles in most locations, but this is what you can expect to taste from the various regions. "These flavors come from the altitude, climate, and soil on which the coffee is grown, based on the nutrients and surrounding plant life" (MacDonnell, 1). For example, coffee from some farms in Thailand has a distinct macadamia undertone since the coffee trees are grown in the shade of macadamia trees. Chocolatey flavors come from nearby cacao trees, and fruity flavors can come from the coffee bean remaining in the coffee cherry as it dries.

For many, these flavor profiles may not be easy to detect. Casual coffee drinkers do not take a sip of coffee and say, 'Mmmmm, tastes like pineapple!' because the notes are subtle. Much in the same way that casual wine drinkers cannot taste oaky tones when sipping wine. It takes practice and patience to pinpoint these flavors, but the ones you do can elevate your coffee experience. Understanding the flavor notes can help you find quality coffee; it pays to remember that old coffee can quickly lose these flavors. After a bit of practice with what you know are quality coffees, you will soon be able to detect when coffee is missing those aromas and be able to select your coffee more carefully.

Another way to narrow down what coffee is best for you is by pairing it with your brewing method. The next chapter will establish some of the most popular brewing methods you can do at home, but each will bring different mouthfeels and flavors to your coffee. Some types of coffee work better with particular brewing methods than others, so matching them can make it a bit easier to shop in the future. It can be like pairing wine and cheese; they are all great individually, but it can change your world when you put the right combination together. You can start with your favorite method or region and work from there.

Pressurized coffee is usually a quick energy-packed process and can extract deep flavors in a short amount of time. Because of the speed of these processes, medium-to-dark roasts are generally better as these beans have a more concentrated flavor. You do not want to lose the great qualities of coffee through this process, so stronger roasts work well for this method. Pressurized coffee brewing methods include devices like the Espresso Machine, Stovetop Moka Pot, and the AeroPress. Kenyan coffee is an excellent option for these methods. If you prefer to steep your coffee, such as with a French Press or a Siphon, medium-bodied dark roasts are a great option to get all of the complex flavors into your cup. Because steeping takes longer than pressurizing the coffee, it has the time to absorb more of the coffee's essence. So, with darker, more flavorful roasts, you can taste the complex pallet of flavors and appreciate the coffee more. African and South American coffees complement well with immersion techniques. The tried-and-true method of filtration, or the pour-over method, works well for most coffee types. The hot water has enough time to seep through the grounds but not too long to risk becoming bitter. If you prefer pour-over coffee, medium roasts from Central America are perfect for this method. Central American coffees are grown in similar cultures that participate in similar growing practices, so they have a common thread of flavor. Filtration brings out the right amount of flavor with medium roast beans because there is not too much flavor that you miss out on in this process and avoids the coffee becoming too watery.

One more final thing to note when considering the dimensions of coffee in your purchasing choices is its storage. Coffee flavors rely on freshness, which is why the forgotten coffee in the back of your cabinet tastes bitter. "Buying fresh coffee is one of the best ways to know it is good coffee. Supermarkets often have old coffee on the shelves that sit and wait to be purchased for weeks" (Home grounds, 1). This coffee is not as good as freshly-roasted coffee. You can begin by purchasing fresh coffee, but you must also keep it fresh in your home. Storing the coffee in air-sealed bags in a cool area and away from sunlight is the best way to avoid it losing its quality. If you like to buy in bulk, you can extend your coffee's freshness by freezing it for a month. This is a great way to ensure it does not get too old while finishing your current coffee bag. Purchasing whole beans and grinding them yourself is another great tip for keeping your coffee as fresh as possible. Grinders are relatively inexpensive and easy to use, so try grinding a fresh cup of coffee every morning to enhance flavors.

Coffee Features To Know

Since coffee is a huge industry, each brand or company has tried to create wording or stickers to make their coffee stand out among the rest. Catchy words like organic, supremo, or AA coffee do mean something concerning the quality of the coffee but can be thrown on the bags haphazardly. Getting the hang of what these terms mean and how they relate to the coffee can help lessen the confusion and show you what you are purchasing. A disclaimer to this notion is that there are many grading systems qualifying coffee and not one universal group. Some cheap brands will slap catchy words onto their bags without any evidence to back up their meaning. It is not chronic but something to be aware of as you learn about these terms.

There are grading systems in place for every region where coffee is grown, and although the specifics may differ, "there are still general practices" (Trabocca, 1). Grading coffee beans looks at their size, how many defective beans there are in a measured amount, and how the coffee tastes: Kenya and other African countries grade beans based on a letter system. "AA is the largest and highest quality of beans and can be sold at a higher price" (Ospina, 1). The smaller the beans, the lower their letter grading; the letters go from AA, A, B, C, and PB.

Colombia uses a two-term grading system. Supremo beans are the best quality while Excelso is the lower quality. These two systems are the biggest and most easily recognized. Many countries use a number system, but you are less likely to see these grades on labels, as it is less well known. If there is one that interests you, it is better to search that term and that country specifically to understand what the grading means. Since each country grades differently, there is no simple way to access the best grades. Still, if you see an AA or Supremo title on coffee from the corresponding countries, you are headed in the right direction.

Certifications are also a big part of producers trying to sell their coffee and stand out. Again, there are many certifications out there, but there are a few you should be aware of. If you are from the USA, you may be familiar with the USDA Certified Organic. "Coffees with this certification mean that the coffee was grown on a farm that did not use chemicals, and preferred natural growing processes in its production" (RoyalCup, 1). Be careful with the 'organic' term because distributors can put it in any part of their promotion, but it does not mean the coffee was grown organically. Please do not trust the word itself; instead, believe the certification. "Another is the Fairtrade Certification, which ensures that the farmers and workers who grew the coffee were treated fairly with wages and working hours" (RoyalCup, 1). As most coffee production happens in third-world countries, big coffee-producing companies will abuse the workers by not providing basic amenities and forcing long working days for little-to-no pay. Fairtrade coffee ensures this does not happen to workers and helps farms be environmentally sustainable.

Coffee growing practices can destroy habitats, endangering delicate ecosystems; intentional organizations can help mitigate and protect the land coffee is growing on; "the Smithsonian Bird Friendly Certifications is just one of these" (RoyalCup, 1). As trees are clear-cut to plant coffee trees to meet global demand, birds are left homeless with nowhere to go. This seal means that the coffee was organic and shade-grown, which is better for the birds and the quality of the coffee itself. The Rainforest Alliance Certification is another excellent option to support as they work in favor of everyone. "This organization ensures the coffee beans, biodiversity, and farmers within the coffee growing process are treated sustainably" (RoyalCup, 1). You may see other certifications, but these are the more popular and credible ones.

Buying from Roasters

As mentioned before, fresh coffee is one of the main principles you should be looking for as you buy quality coffee. The fancy bag on the shelf may have been incredible when first roasted, but it loses many of its qualities after sitting for weeks. There are several ways to find fresh coffee, and it is rarely from a grocery store. Local roasters are likely the best way to find the freshest coffee available to you. Freshness relies more upon the freshness of the roast than when the beans were harvested. Now, of course, if the beans were harvested, roasted, and consumed close together, there is little comparison. Once the coffee is roasted, its shelf life dwindles bit by bit. Local roasters buy unprocessed green coffee beans from suppliers and roast them accordingly. It is a unique craft that roasters take pride in, so your best bet to find fresh coffee is to find a local roaster and purchase from them; consider the size of their facility and bean varieties. Good roasters will usually have rotating imports, so new coffees will become available to try, and your favorites are always in stock.

With no local roasters nearby, some people feel doomed to have lower-quality coffee than others. Luckily our time is blessed with the gifts of universal trade and the internet. Online roasters are a popular option for getting high-quality fresh coffee. Because of online platforms, they usually have more flexibility and can hold more bean varieties; you can discover new coffees from the comfort of your sofa. One significant thing to note about online roasters is checking that they roast the coffee beans after ordering. This will ensure the freshness of the roast you are purchasing and keep you from paying for out-of-date coffee sitting in storage. Many roasters work to ensure this does not happen, but keep this in mind as you look for fresh coffee beans.

If you are still unsure what coffee you like, a subscription is a great way to try out different flavor profiles worldwide, helping you experiment and find your favorite. Some programs have questionnaires that allow you to customize your selection. Others have more selective processes and only send out certain coffees each month; this method ensures the freshness of the roasted bean, as it is typically sent directly after roasting. This is an excellent way to start your journey of enlightenment into the complex world of coffee, as it allows you to try excellent quality coffee without overthinking.

Buying coffee may seem overwhelming as you begin to learn about the complexity of the whole system. With so many options, flavors, varieties, and grades, one can easily get lost in the coffee world. It is essential to determine which combination works best for you, but it should not be a chore. The experimental nature of finding your favorites leads to trying many new coffee styles and knowledge you had never experienced before. Here are the principles to know as you buy your next bag of coffee:

1. Understand the flavors involved with your coffee. If you like your coffee naturally sweeter or thicker, this will help you determine the country and roast.

2. Know what consistency you want. Knowing how you like your coffee and how the flavors interact will guide your choices into the right combination.

3. Buy it fresh. Whether through a local or online roaster or a subscription program, fresh coffee is the best coffee, and you will not regret being selective.

Most of all, try as much as you can! You may not think you like chocolatey coffee until you find the perfect bag from a small farm in the mountains of Guatemala. Enjoying coffee is about enjoying the journey and growing your coffee-tasting pallet, not finding the perfect coffee every time.

CHAPTER 5

MAKING COFFEE GREAT

"Numbing sensation on the tip of the tongue"

There is nothing better than sitting at your table in the morning, the smell of rich coffee filling the air, and sipping on a cup of coffee that alerts your mind and soothes your soul. To some, all coffee might taste the same. But to those who love the drink and constantly seek out ways to find the best brew, you will be familiar with different forms of coffee, such as the classic coffee

maker or your favorite latte. Even with those reasonable options to get your morning coffee intake, it can be satisfying and exciting to look for other ways to make a better cup of coffee at home without running to the nearest cafe.

Luckily, there have been a few hundred years for people to invent and perfect the act of coffee consumption. There are so many ways to make coffee, some more traditional methods and others more modern. For example, many are familiar with the coffee pot maker that sits on any kitchen or workplace counter. But you may not know that one way of consuming coffee in Turkey involves drawing a small metal cup of a coffee mixture over hot sand till it boils and becomes a small espresso-like coffee drink. It creates a thick, rich blend of bitter coffee that people have loved for centuries before the creation of instant coffee.

If you are looking to up your coffee game at home, this sand-heating method will probably not work for you. Still, there are an incredible number of options to make coffee in any form you prefer. You can let coffee slowly drip from a filter, extracting all the benefits from the beans. You can make it as frontier Americans did by boiling coffee beans and water together before filtering it out. Or, you can embrace modernity and pressurize the mixture to get a dark and robust coffee. Here, we will examine just a few ways to make your at-home coffee better than you thought you could.

What Makes Good Coffee?

Before we look into the different ways to make coffee at home, it is helpful to understand the different identifiable elements of coffee that you may not be familiar with. Coffee is like any other drink or food we consume, and preferences depend on each person. It may seem challenging to identify which coffee is the best, but coffee connoisseurs have developed a ranking system to help distinguish the quality of different beans. They look at coffee beans based on their acidity, body, mouthfeel, and flavor profile, all dependent on the climate and location from which the beans are grown. The coffee tree is also susceptible to these factors, and the coffee beans produced taste different based on these conditions. Altitude comes into play when determining the quality of the beans too. "Coffee grown in higher altitudes is considered higher quality because the coffee beans ripen slower than those in lower altitudes, making a richer flavor profile" (Pebble & Pine, 1).

Acidity is one of the more easily identifiable elements of coffee. "It has nothing to do with actual acid or the pH of the coffee" (Wilhem, 1). "Sometimes the acidity of coffee is described as the pleasing sharpness felt at the front of the mouth, a numbing sensation on the tip of the tongue, or dryness at the back of the palate and/or under the edges of the tongue" (Wilhem, 1). The acidity also describes the other flavors of coffee, whether it is sweet, citrusy, or chocolatey; for example, the body of coffee often describes how the coffee feels in your mouth, not just the overall flavors. "There are three categories; light, medium, and full-bodied" (Coffee Community, 1). A full-bodied coffee often feels thick or heavy in your mouth and is created mainly in volcanic and high-altitude locations, such as Guatemala. Light body coffees are usually grown in soils with lower nutrients, resulting in less residue when sipped. Medium body coffees are a blend of the two. Acidity and body are affected by the roast of the coffee, which is why some coffees are better with a light roast than others.

Each bag of coffee you buy will have differing degrees of these elements to make a unique brew. Understanding how these coffee aspects work together can help you find your favorite brand, or at least help you understand artisanal coffee a bit more. You must have heard people say that cooking your food makes it more meaningful to eat; well, knowing where your morning coffee was grown and the best way to drink it can add more satisfaction to your enjoyment. There are many ways to brew your coffee to perfection. We will examine some of the most popular at-home ways to diversify your coffee habits and develop your relationship with the beverage by looking at the brewing process, the good elements this brings, and its downsides.

Drip Method

One of the most common ways for people to brew coffee is through the drip method, also known as the pour-over method. It is simple and easy and can make a great cup of coffee. There are endless machines to buy that brew coffee with this method; it is likely sitting somewhere in your kitchen right now. However, these machines are a simplified version and do not deliver the subtle flavors of many coffee grounds, there are drip methods that can provide that perfect coffee with all the subtle flavors, but these take precision and are mastered over time. Essentially, the drip method is straightforward. The coffee is placed in a filter over a cup or coffee pot, and hot water is slowly placed on top of the grounds. Gravity drags the water through the coffee grounds, absorbing the coffee and falling through the filter into the cup. The machines that you can find cheap that use this method distributes the water in splattered intervals and in an uneven fashion, which can result in the coffee not being absorbed as well as it could. You can use this same method with special brewing equipment while creating better coffee. If you make sure the grounds in the filter are evenly distributed and very gently pour the hot water in a controlled manner, you can get a flavorful and fruity cup of coffee.

There are many benefits to this method. The coffee filter ensures that you will have a very clean cup of coffee, with no grounds to chew on as you enjoy it! Drip coffee's calming and simple practice can also make it a great show for guests, as you can show off your coffee expertise visually and serve your guests a beautifully- crafted cup of coffee. It is also an excellent method for single-origin coffee, as it brings out all the flavors of coffee. Specifically, the way this method brings out coffee flavors is a perfect option for floral light roast coffees. This method can bring out the subtle notes within, so that you can taste the flavors labeled on the packages.

Practicing this method at the same level as the professionals takes a lot of precision and patience. The drip method can be technical and time-consuming if you want to get the perfect cup. "Many baristas use a scale to help make the coffee and water measurements perfectly exact" (Soque, 1). It also requires specific instruments, good filters, and the right movements to come out in its best form. Since pouring water over the coffee grounds needs to be done by hand, this leaves much room for human error. You can never really guarantee that each cup is going to taste the same. If you use a machine to make the coffee that wakes you up in the morning, you are probably satisfied to get a simple caffeine boost. But if you want to play around with coffee brewing a bit more and try your hand at the artisanal craft, the drip method is a quality classic.

French Press

The French Press is an interesting yet straightforward method of coffee brewing, and can be one of the easiest ways to get as much flavor out of coffee grounds as possible. Some coffee houses have a set up where you can order a French Press instead of a pot of coffee, so you can steep it and pour it to your liking. Depending on whom you ask, the French Press may not even be French. There are many patents out there for the basic design. "The first iteration of the one you may be familiar with was developed in 1929 by Italians named Attilio Calimani and Giulio Moneta" (Solano, 1). The French Press method is a fully-immersive coffee-brewing idea, where the coarse grounds are steeped in almost-boiling water to extract all the flavors and oils from the coffee. The compact machine comprises a glass or metal basin, where you place your grounds in the bottom and pour hot water over the top. After stirring the mixture a few times, place the plunger just above the water; the coffee can be steeped in the water. After three to four minutes, slowly press the plunger until all the grounds have been filtered and pressed to the bottom. Now the coffee is ready to enjoy in any way you like!

The French Press is a favorite among many coffee drinkers, as it is easier than many other methods. It doesn't require expensive equipment and can make any coffee taste rich. Because the coffee grounds sit in the water and the water isn't pulled out quickly by gravity, the coffee produced is thicker and more full-bodied. If you like your coffee as dark as it can be, this method is excellent while achieving great flavors. If several people in your household love coffee, this method is ideal for making it in bulk. Depending on the size of the French Press, you can serve several cups at once, whereas other methods are more individual. The compact setup of the French Press does not take up much space on your kitchen counter; there is no need to juggle different instruments to make a simple coffee.

The clean-up method can be a bit messy. Since there is no disposable filter that catches the grounds, you have to be diligent about cleaning your French Press if you do not have a garbage disposal. It also needs to be consumed quickly after brewing to get the best flavor from a French Press. Letting the grounds sit for a long time will only extract more and more bitter flavors from the coffee grounds, making it less enjoyable. Due to this, you must clean well after each use. Most presses have mesh filters that are simple to take apart for cleaning, but if grounds get stuck, they may mess up the flavors of your next coffee.

Stovetop Moka Pot

If you like espresso coffee every morning without the expense of purchasing an espresso machine, a Stovetop Moka Pot may be perfect! "The Stovetop Pot originated in Italy as a product of the growing coffee culture in the 1800s" (Storr, 1) to make the expensive process of espresso cheaper for the common folk. Alfonso Bialetti created the Moka Pot we love today. It was named after the famous coffee port in Yemen, where coffee was traded and exported to Europe for centuries. This system carries the same principles as espresso but can be done from any stovetop, as hot steam is pressurized through the coffee grounds to make a thick creamy coffee. The Stovetop Moka Pot has three parts:

- A lower chamber where the water is placed and heated.

- A middle chamber for the coffee grounds.

- And an upper chamber for the brewed coffee.

The boiling water from the bottom chamber makes steam; the pressure of the steam forces the hot water up the funnel and through the coffee grounds and into the top chamber producing a full-bodied, rich coffee that does not have a burnt or metallic taste.

It can be fun experimenting with a Stovetop Pot, such as making thick coffee! Some people have made lattes with this device while frothing warm milk with a French Press plunger, but you can also play with water-to-coffee ratios to find the right combination. You can also add chocolate to this process to create a Mocha or add water to the coffee to make an Americano. Like the French Press, this device is relatively simple and easy to use. It can take time to nail down the brewing process of the Stovetop Moka Pot, but a bit of tinkering does not take away from the deliciousness of the result. It takes a bit more love than other methods to ensure the process is correct, but it can be an excellent method if you love rich coffee. Or, if you are like the Italians who fell in love with this invention or maybe just looking for a cheaper alternative to make some look-alike espresso!

Espresso

Anyone who has heard of coffee has heard of espresso. The famous thick and bitter coffee originates, once again, from Italy. "Luigi Bezzara created the first espresso machine in 1901, which quickly took off and became a favorite brewing method all over Europe" (Greaves, 1). The machine is complex, with multiple mechanisms working together to make espresso. The process involves:

- Steaming water.

- Warming it to just before boiling point.

- Pushing it through compact coffee grounds.

The concept sounds simple but is challenging to perfect and takes lots of skill to do well; the coffee grounds must be evenly distributed, then evenly and smoothly pressed down before being placed into the espresso machine; all to avoid channeling, which is where the water will find the path of least resistance as it falls through the grounds. It can create an uneven flavor profile and prevent the espresso from becoming rich and smooth. When done correctly, the result is a thick and tangy shot of espresso full of deep flavor and complex aromas.

Espresso machines can make a fuller and more decadent coffee than a French Press as the drink is more condensed. It is also excellent at expressing the various flavors and aromas of coffee - a technical, beautiful masterpiece of man and machine delivering perfection when the symphony is in harmony. The versatility of espresso shots is probably its most famous quality. Espresso is delicious to drink straight or with cream, diluted in water as an Americano, or combined with warm milk and syrups to create a myriad of fun sweet drinks. However, making an espresso yourself can be a pretty strenuous process. It is a skill that professional baristas work hard to master, so much so that it is the subject of several competitions. A quality machine can also be expensive, and with much work involved to make espresso, most are happy to go to a cafe instead. If you are just starting your coffee journey or are a little more developed, you will enjoy the flavors of espresso-made coffee. Just know that it is not as easy to make as it may seem!

Siphon

For many, brewing coffee with a standard coffee pot or even a French Press is an exciting and mouth-watering endeavor. Yet, we're not satisfied and wanted to find a fresh way to create quality coffee. Those who enjoy waking up to a science experiment before their morning coffee may fall in love with the Siphon method. "The Siphon originated in Germany around the 1830s" (Jones, 1) as people were fed up with their coffee tasting bitter. This is a mix between the French Press and the Stovetop methods, as the coffee is fully immersed using pressure from steam to force the water upwards. Essentially, the hot water in the boiling pot at the bottom of the Siphon heats up until the water is forced upwards in a tube to meet the coffee grounds; the mixed water and coffee grounds cool, where gravity brings it back down through a filter, removing the grounds and leaving just the coffee. The Siphon method brings out the best flavor of the coffee through immersion while also making it full-bodied and thicker than other methods.

The downsides to the Siphon are the cleaning process and the specific equipment needed to pull it off. Because of the awkward shape of the Siphon, it is difficult to clean thoroughly, and has several parts to reassemble afterward. The process is not simple; you need to be dedicated to using it frequently. But still, it was created out of a need for better coffee, and it delivers on this front. You get many of the benefits of various other coffee-making methods through a very eye-catching process. If you want to show off incredible coffee to your friends with a dazzling presentation, the Siphon takes the cake! Is it practical for everyday use? Not really.

AeroPress

The AeroPress is one of the newest methods of coffee brewing that has taken the world by storm. So much so that there are competitions to find who can use it best! It was created in 2005 by the leader of a toy-making company, Alan Adler. This origin story led to much doubt in its early years, but it has since become fully embraced by the coffee community due to its smooth taste and efficiency. Adler went to one of his engineers because he wanted to reduce the bitterness of his coffee, which is achieved through less brewing time. It is a fast process that has created award-winning coffee. The AeroPress comprises just two small cylinders that utilize human pressure to push water and coffee through a filter into the final product; that's it! There are many recipes out there to help you make different coffee to complement different varieties, as well as an inverted method that changes the composition of the coffee. These processes are the same and come down to preference and coffee brand, but either way makes a refined French Press coffee quicker and easier to handle.

There are many benefits to the AeroPress; for one, it is compact and straightforward. It will not take up a lot of storing space and is easy to clean. The versatility of the AeroPress is what makes it stand out; if you like the fuller body of a French Press brew or the lighter aroma of a pour-over. "You can achieve these with different grounds, water temperatures, and brewing times" (Guevara, 1); the AeroPress allows you to experiment with your coffee - this method is very forgiving and will mostly produce a good coffee and often come out incredibly. This device is also the most portable of all coffee makers with its small size. You can bring it with you as you travel or camp, so you never have to leave your favorite coffee behind. The biggest drawback of the AeroPress is that you can only make one cup per rotation. It's a compact size, so if you want to make coffee for two or enjoy a top-up, this is not the best method. Like many other methods discussed, it takes practice and may take several attempts when following recipes. Overall, this new update to coffee brewing is easy once mastered, delightful, and versatile in so many ways.

Conclusion

Making coffee great is a craft that speaks to each person differently. Combining coffee brewing science and flavor profile can make each cup unique. There are excellent methods for entertaining others, and some are perfect just for you. With no natural way to find the all-time best coffee brewing method, there seems to be no point in ranking a Stovetop to an AeroPress because there is no one-hat-fits-all at the end of the day. Finding ways that you enjoy in both the process and the resulting coffee is essential in making the coffee great for you. Some artisanal coffee shops may have these methods available for you to try, while others you may have to seek out in different ways. The coffee world is old and complex, leaving plenty of room for each coffee connoisseur to discover their favorite cup of coffee and enjoy the journey along the way.

Carl Mainwaring

COFFEE

ACKNOWLEDGEMENT

Maureen Gwendalen Jolley (born)

To all of those very precious mothers and mothers to be, but primarily to my special mother, Maureen. Who sees the best in me even when the best of me has taken a vacation? Who believed in me? Without your unconditional love and belief, this publication would not have been possible; to all you sons and daughters, treasure every second you have with your mother and never be afraid to show your love.

COFFEE

REFERENCE NOTES

CHAPTER 1 REFERENCES: HISTORY OF COFFEE HOUSES

Bigirimana, B. (2014, October 15). In Kaldi's footsteps: A journey to the birthplace of coffee. World Bank. Retrieved February 7, 2022, from https://www.worldbank.org/en/news/feature/2014/10/07/in-kaldis-footsteps-a-journey-to-the-birthplace-of-coffee

Brooks, J. (2019, September 14). When Frederick the Great went to war on coffee. Brookston Beer Bulletin. Retrieved February 12, 2022, from https://brookstonbeerbulletin.com/when-frederick-the-great-went-to-war-on-coffee/

Gamm, N. (2014, December 27). Coffee and coffeehouses among the Ottomans. Hürriyet Daily News. Retrieved February 7, 2022, from https://www.hurriyetdailynews.com/coffee-and-coffeehouses-among-the-ottomans-76123

Kovick, M. (2020, October 1). The history of Coffee Culture in Italy. Wanted in Rome. Retrieved February 11, 2022, from https://www.wantedinrome.com/news/why-italians-are-obsessed-with-coffee-the-history-of-coffee-culture-in-italy.html

Rotondi, J. P. (2020, February 11). How coffee-fueled revolutions-and changed history. History.com. Retrieved January 24, 2022, from https://www.history.com/news/coffee-houses-revolutions

Ramjattan, B. (2020, June 2). The history of Coffee Houses and cafe culture. Coffee or Die Magazine. Retrieved January 24, 2022, from https://coffeeordie.com/coffee-house-cafe-culture/

Rosenberg, F. (2020, August 14). A history of coffee: The Old World Obsession. WE THE ORIGIN. Retrieved February 8, 2022, from https://wetheorigin.com/coffee-culture/a-history-of-coffee-the-old-world-obsession/

Smith, C. (2021, August 24). Café de la Paix. History Hit. Retrieved February 11, 2022, from https://www.historyhit.com/locations/cafe-de-la-paix/

Suter, K. (2005). The rise and fall of English coffee houses. Contemporary Review, 286(1669), 107-110. https://www.csun.edu/~kaddison/suter.pdf

CHAPTER 2 REFERENCES: COFFEE AND POLYPHENOL

Bjarnadottir, A. (2019, February 20). Coffee and antioxidants: Everything you need to know. Healthline. Retrieved March 1,

2022, from https://www.healthline.com/nutrition/coffee-worlds-biggest-source-of-antioxidants

Fukagawa, S., Haramizu, S., Sasaoka, S., Yasuda, Y., Tsujimura, H., & Murase, T. (2017). Coffee polyphenols extracted from green coffee beans improve skin properties and microcirculatory function. Bioscience, Biotechnology, and Biochemistry, 81(9), 1814–1822. https://doi.org/10.1080/09168451.2017.1345614

Gunnars, K. (2018, May 4). Can coffee increase your metabolism and help you burn fat? Healthline. Retrieved March 2, 2022, from https://www.healthline.com/nutrition/coffee-increase-metabolism

Hermansen, K., Krogholm, K. S., Bech, B. H., Dragsted, L. O., Hyldstrup, L., Jørgensen, K., Larsen, M. L., & Tjønneland, A. M. (2012). Kaffe kan beskytte mod sygdom [Coffee can protect against disease]. Ugeskrift for laeger, 174(39), 2293–2297.

Ishida, K., Yamamoto, M., Misawa, K., Nishimura, H., Misawa, K., Ota, N., & Shimotoyodome, A. (2019). Coffee polyphenols prevent cognitive dysfunction and suppress amyloid β plaques in APP/PS2 transgenic mice. Neuroscience Research, 154, 35–44. https://doi.org/10.1016/j.neures.2019.05.001

Król, K., Gantner, M., Tatarak, A., & Hallmann, E. (2019). The content of polyphenols in coffee beans as roasting, origin, and storage effect. European Food Research and Technology, 246(1), 33–39. https://doi.org/10.1007/s00217-019-03388-9

Llczbiński, P., & Bukowska, B. (2021). Tea and coffee polyphenols and their biological properties are based on the latest in vitro investigations. Industrial Crops and Products, 175, 114265. https://doi.org/10.1016/j.indcrop.2021.114265

Mendes, E. (2018, April 3). Coffee and cancer: What the research shows. American Cancer Society. Retrieved March 2, 2022, from https://www.cancer.org/latest-news/coffee-and-cancer-what-the-research-really-shows.html

Murase, T., Misawa, K., Minegishi, Y., Aoki, M., Ominami, H., Suzuki, Y., Shibuya, Y., & Hase, T. (2010). Coffee polyphenols suppress diet-induced body fat accumulation by down-regulating SREBP-1C and related molecules in C57BL/6J MICE. American Journal of Physiology-Endocrinology and Metabolism, 300(1). https://doi.org/10.1152/ajpendo.00441.2010

Petre, A. (2019, July 8). What are polyphenols? Types, benefits, and food sources. Healthline. Retrieved March 1, 2022, from https://www.healthline.com/nutrition/polyphenols#what-they-are

CHAPTER 3 REFERENCES: WORLD ATLAS OF COFFEE

Blue Coffee Box. (2018, June 26). Which countries grow the Best South American Coffee? Coffee School - Blue Coffee Box. Retrieved February 22, 2022, from https://learn.bluecoffeebox.com/countries-grow-best-south-american-coffee/

Castellano, N. (2021, November 1). How does El Niño affect coffee production? Perfect Daily Grind. Retrieved February 22,

2022, from https://perfectdailygrind.com/2021/09/how-does-el-nino-affect-coffee-production/

Espresso & Coffee Guide. (2020, October 16). Kenya Coffee Beans. Espresso & Coffee Guide. Retrieved February 23, 2022, from https://espressocoffeeguide.com/gourmet-coffee/arabian-and-african-coffees/kenya-coffee/

Espresso & Coffee Guide. (2020, October 16). Uganda Coffee Beans. Espresso & Coffee Guide. Retrieved February 23, 2022, from https://espressocoffeeguide.com/gourmet-coffee/arabian-and-african-coffees/uganda-coffee/

Espresso International. (n.d.). Asian coffee varieties " Unique coffee culture • kopi luvac. Espresso International. Retrieved February 23, 2022, from https://www.espresso-international.com/asia-coffee/

Felongco, P. (2021, July 11). African Coffee Beans: The ultimate 2022 guide. Sip Coffee House. Retrieved February 23, 2022, from https://sipcoffeehouse.com/african-coffee/

Halo. (2020, May 25). Coffee regions: A quick guide to coffee growing regions. Halo Coffee. Retrieved February 20, 2022, from https://halo.coffee/blogs/discover/coffee-regions-a-quick-guide-to-coffee-growing-regions

Kahn, C. (2014, July 28). Rust devastates Guatemala's prime coffee crop and its farmers. NPR. Retrieved February 19, 2022, from https://www.npr.org/sections/thesalt/2014/07/28/335293974/rust-devastates-guatemalas-prime-coffee-crop-and-its-farmers

Khan, S. A. (2020, February 14). Reform in Saudi Arabia: The climate-coffee connection. Scientific American Blog Network. Retrieved February 22, 2022, from https:// blogs.scientificamerican.com/observations/reform-in-saudi-arabia-the-climate-coffee-connection/

Mungai, C. (2015, October 22). Which African countries produce the most coffee? World Economic Forum. Retrieved February 23, 2022, from https://www.weforum.org/agenda/2015/10/which-african-countries-produce-the-most-coffee/

NCA. (n.d.). National Coffee Association. National Coffee Association USA. Retrieved February 23, 2022, from https:// www.ncausa.org/About-Coffee/Coffee-Around-the-World

Neighborhood. (2020, October 30). What's South American coffee like? Neighbourhood Coffee Roasters. Retrieved February 20, 2022, from https:// www.neighbourhoodcoffee.co.uk/faq/whats-south-american-coffee-like/

Ospina, A. K. M. (2022, January 26). Kenya AA, Colombia supremo: Understanding coffee grading. Perfect Daily Grind. Retrieved February 22, 2022, from https://perfectdailygrind.com/ 2018/11/kenya-aa-colombia-supremo-understanding-coffee-grading/

Tark, S. H. (2020, July 20). Understanding the Middle East's flourishing coffee market. Perfect Daily Grind. Retrieved February 22, 2022, from https://perfectdailygrind.com/2020/06/ understanding-the-middle-easts-flourishing-coffee-market/

Pebble & Pine, C. (n.d.). Ultimate Guide to Central American Coffee. Pebble & Pine Coffee. Retrieved February 18, 2022, from https://pebbleandpine.co.uk/pages/ultimate-guide-central-american-coffee

Queen Bean, T. (2019, September 11). Regional Coffee Profile: Central America. Coffee with the Queen. Retrieved February 18, 2022, from https://thequeenbean.blog/2018/03/28/regional-coffee-profile-central-america/

Queen Bean. (2020, June 28). Regional Coffee Profile: Asia. Coffee with the Queen. Retrieved February 23, 2022, from https://thequeenbean.blog/2018/06/08/regional-coffee-profile-asia/

Reini, J. (2019, January 1). Costa Rica's 30 Year Ban on Robusta Coffee Trees. Today by the Numbers. Retrieved February 18, 2022, from https://todaybythenumbers.com/2018/11/costa-ricas-30-year-ban-on-robusta-coffee-trees.html

CHAPTER 4 REFERENCES: BUYING COFFEE

Azoury, A. (2022, February 25). Best coffee beans in the world (and a foolproof tip for choosing). Home Grounds. Retrieved February 27, 2022, from https://www.homegrounds.co/best-coffee-beans-bucket-list/

MacDonnell, K. (2022, January 9). What is Fruity Coffee? Tasting notes & tips! Coffee Affection. Retrieved February 27, 2022, from https://coffeeaffection.com/what-is-fruity-coffee/

Ospina, A. K. M. (2022, January 26). Kenya AA, Colombia supremo: Understanding coffee grading. Perfect Daily Grind. Retrieved February 27, 2022, from https://perfectdailygrind.com/2018/11/kenya-aa-colombia-supremo-understanding-coffee-grading/

RoyalCup. (2017, March 30). What do coffee certifications mean? Royal Cup Coffee. Retrieved February 27, 2022, from https://www.royalcupcoffee.com/blog/articles/what-do-coffee-certifications-really-mean

Trabocca. (2021, March 17). Coffee grades: Understanding the basics. Trabocca. Retrieved February 27, 2022, from https://www.trabocca.com/coffee-knowledge/quality/coffee-grades-understanding-the-basics/

West Coast Chefs. (n.d.). Pairing regional beans with brewing methods. West Coast Chef. Retrieved February 27, 2022, from https://thewestcoastchef.com/pairing-regional-beans-with-brewing-methods/

CHAPTER 5 RESOURCES: MAKING COFFEE GREAT

Addict, C. (2021, October 25). 8 popular different ways to make coffee at home. Full Coffee Roast. Retrieved February 24, 2022, from https://fullcoffeeroast.com/different-ways-to-make-coffee/

Community Coffee. (n.d.). Coffee 101: The Body. Coffee 101: The body. Retrieved February 18, 2022, from https://www.communitycoffee.com/blog/detail/coffee-101-the-body

Greaves, E. (2021, February 10). A short history of the Italian espresso. Perfect Daily Grind. Retrieved February 26, 2022, from https://perfectdailygrind.com/2016/04/the-history-of-italian-espresso-do-you-know-your-coffee-history/

Guevara, J. (2021, March 6). AeroPress Coffee Guide: How to brew for different flavor profiles. Perfect Daily Grind. Retrieved February 26, 2022, from https://perfectdailygrind.com/2017/08/aeropress-coffee-guide-how-to-brew-for-different-flavor-profiles/

Jones, J. (2022, February 10). Vacpot Syphon: The History & Brewing Guide. Perfect Daily Grind. Retrieved February 26, 2022, from https://perfectdailygrind.com/2015/10/vacpot-syphon-the-history-brewing-guide/

Prinsloo, M. (2022, January 19). The history of the AeroPress, from concept to championships. Perfect Daily Grind. Retrieved February 26, 2022, from https://perfectdailygrind.com/2019/03/the-history-of-the-aeropress-from-concept-to-championships/

Solano, F. (2021, March 6). French press - The History & Brewing Guide. Perfect Daily Grind. Retrieved February 26, 2022, from https://perfectdailygrind.com/2015/05/french-press-the-history-brewing-guide/

Soque, N. (2019, January 25). Everything you need to know to brew great pour-over coffee ... Perfect Daily Grind. Retrieved February 26, 2022, from https://perfectdailygrind.com/2019/01/everything-you-need-to-know-to-brew-great-filter-pour-over-drip-coffee/

Storr, T. (2020, April 27). How the Moka Pot influenced coffee consumption. Perfect Daily Grind. Retrieved February 26, 2022, from https://perfectdailygrind.com/2019/11/how-the-moka-pot-influenced-coffee-consumption/

Wilhelm, A. (2021, June 15). What is coffee acidity? Verena Street Coffee Co. Retrieved February 18, 2022, from https://www.verenastreet.com/blogs/all-about-coffee/what-is-coffee-acidity

Carl Mainwaring

COFFEE

ABOUT THE AUTHOR

Carl Mainwaring is a British/New Zealander living in Auckland, New Zealand. His goals in life are simple— to be the husband of a rock star primary school teacher and the dedicated father of two beautiful young children. Carl, an enthusiastic coffee lover, along with his thirst for knowledge, made 'Coffee' a natural choice for his debut book, conceived while in the solitude of nature at his sunny North Auckland home surrounded by ancient forest.

COFFEE